YOUR KNOWLEDGE HAS VALUE

- We will publish your bachelor's and master's thesis, essays and papers

- Your own eBook and book - sold worldwide in all relevant shops

- Earn money with each sale

Upload your text at www.GRIN.com
and publish for free

Bibliographic information published by the German National Library:

The German National Library lists this publication in the National Bibliography; detailed bibliographic data are available on the Internet at http://dnb.dnb.de .

This book is copyright material and must not be copied, reproduced, transferred, distributed, leased, licensed or publicly performed or used in any way except as specifically permitted in writing by the publishers, as allowed under the terms and conditions under which it was purchased or as strictly permitted by applicable copyright law. Any unauthorized distribution or use of this text may be a direct infringement of the author s and publisher s rights and those responsible may be liable in law accordingly.

Imprint:

Copyright © 2017 GRIN Verlag
Print and binding: Books on Demand GmbH, Norderstedt Germany
ISBN: 9783668640016

This book at GRIN:

https://www.grin.com/document/412342

Tim Wenninger

"Special Economics" by Maureen McHugh. A contemporary short story worth reading?

An analysis of its qualities and characteristics

GRIN Verlag

GRIN - Your knowledge has value

Since its foundation in 1998, GRIN has specialized in publishing academic texts by students, college teachers and other academics as e-book and printed book. The website www.grin.com is an ideal platform for presenting term papers, final papers, scientific essays, dissertations and specialist books.

Visit us on the internet:

http://www.grin.com/

http://www.facebook.com/grincom

http://www.twitter.com/grin_com

Universität Osnabrück

Term Paper: Cultural and Historical Studies

Seminar: Contemporary Short Stories

Summer semester 2017

Due Date: 15.09.2017

Special Economics – A contemporary short story worth reading?

An analysis of its qualities and characteristics

Tim Wenninger

4. Semester

2-FB: Anglistik und Ev. Theologie

Table of Contents

1. The author: Maureen McHugh 1
2. Summary 1
3. First impression 2
4. Narrative 3
5. Agents and Characters 4
    5.1. Jieling 4
    5.2. Baiyue 5
    5.3. Mr. Wei Rongyi 6
6. Time and Space 6
7. Voice 7
8. Final thoughts 9

1. The author: Maureen McHugh

The author of the short story is an American science fiction and fantasy writer. She was born in Ohio in 1959 and lived most of her life in the United States. Apart from living and working in the US, she has also spent a significant amount of time in China. Taking a look at her works, it can be seen that her life in China has definitely influenced her writings. This influence becomes evident in McHugh's first novel *China Mountain Thang* (1992), in her short story "Special Economics" and in a number of her other works.

Maureen McHugh has not only proved her writing abilities in Special Economics, but already many years prior. In 1993, she won the Locus Award for the best First novel. Three years later, her short story "The Lincoln Train" was awarded with the Hugo and Locus Award for the best short story. It took her 16 more years before she could win her next award. This time she was awarded the Shirley Jackson Award for the best collection of short stories. Her collection of short stories includes the story "Special Economics".

In the following paper, a short overview of the short story itself will be given and more interestingly we will look at the ways in which McHugh's work in the field of interactive fiction has influenced the story and its effect on the reader.

2. Summary

The short story Special Economics takes place in modern China after a big epidemy which has killed one fourth of its population. The story line is built around a 19-year-old girl who has left her family and her home to move to one of China's major cities. There she struggles to make ends meet. Since she does not have a proper job she tries to make some money by dancing and singing on a shabby market. Knowing that this is not a reliable way of income, she is constantly on the lookout for new jobs. Eventually, a job recruiter assigns her to a biotechnology company even though she has almost no qualifications. At first, she is quite happy to have found a job, to eat proper meals, and to sleep in the company's accommodations. But then she meets a rather shy girl who also works for the company and discovers that the company has found a way to secretly enslave the workers so that they cannot leave the company anymore. The two girls come up with a plan to leave the company. They directly put the first step of their plan into action by secretly sneaking out of the company compound one evening. While out in the city they accidentally meet a rather sympathetic man. But as it turns out, the man's motifs were not as pure as the girls might have expected. During an arising conflict, the girls must decide quickly whom to believe and how to act, knowing that their future will depend on it.

3. First impression

My first thoughts were concerned with the way in which the story was written and setup. The style of writing which Maureen McHugh used made it possible to easily read the story and follow its plot. McHugh includes several recognizable themes and patterns which at first evoke the impression of a familiar story. The following are just some examples of these themes and patterns: The poor and young girl moves from a rural area to the big city; the modern youth cannot identify themselves with the traditions and ideologies of the elderly; teenagers face the difficulty of balancing freedom and economic dependencies.

Apart from these familiar elements, however, McHugh included a number of unexpected twists and turns to the plot and its characters. These surprising changes created a suspense which leads to an eager desire to read on and discover more about the plot and its characters. It was for example suspicious and surprising that a young girl without any higher education could get a job at a biotechnology company.

After finishing reading the story, my attention was focused on its underlying message. What did the author try to express and convey by publishing this story? Firstly, I was thinking about the power of large companies and the dependency of its workers. In many cases employees simply accept unjust treatment by their company. This is largely due to the fact that an individual employee feels powerless in face of their companies influence. They therefore often develop the attitude that any kind of effort to improve their situation would be futile nonetheless. However, in this story

Maureen McHugh included a proactive and self-confident protagonist who succeeded in standing up to the intolerable conduct of her company. This resistance might be interpreted as a sign of hope. The expectation that there is always a way in which an unjust situation can be changed and improved.

4. Narrative

Maureen McHugh uses an easy to follow narrative. This becomes evident when the major paragraphs of the stories are being examined. These paragraphs are structured similarly since each of them starts with a description of the scene (setting or time) and is then followed by a dialogue. Apart from the easy to follow narrative, the story also evokes the impression of an exciting and fast-paced story. On the one hand, this impression is created through the plot itself and on the other hand through the use of the third person limited narrator. The plot consists of many different actions that all take place in a short period of time. The use of a few time lapses additionally increases the pace of the story.

Since the story is being told through a third person perspective, the reader only receives information from the protagonist's subjective point of view. In certain situations, during the story, this leads to a lack of information. The reader is compelled to use his or her own imagination to understand the characters' actions, motifs and circumstances.

Considering the three aspects mentioned, it can be concluded that even though the story is fast-paced the reader does not get lost because of its introductory descriptions. Furthermore, McHugh managed to build up suspense and a feeling of rapidity through the plot itself and animates the reader to fill the gaps with his or her creativity and imagination. All this makes the story easy to understand, more exciting and captivating.

5. Agents and Characters

5.1. Jieling

Jieling is a young adult from a smaller sized city in the north west of China and the protagonist of this story. She leaves her family to go to one of China's major cities in the south of China. The reason why she wants to leave does not become completely evident. It is said that she left in order to find a job but if that were the reason, she could have looked for a job in one of the major cities closer to her home. Not much is revealed about her relationship to her family. Her father is dead, her stepfather is friendly, but he also often annoys her. With her mother, she appears to have a somewhat better relationship. When Jieling faces difficult situations, she often wishes to talk to her mother for comfort and advice.

This type of characters might appear familiar to many readers because it can be seen in a number of other stories as well. A young protagonist who leaves his or her home and loved ones to discover the world, to find a better life or to follow whatever personal passion they might have. On their lone journey, these characters often have to face challenges. It is always interesting to look at the way in which a character reacts to these challenges because their behavior reveals much about their personality. In Jieling's case, she acts determined and confident in difficult situations. She is not afraid to take risks and stand up for what she thinks is right. This includes trying to reveal the unjust treatment of the biotechnology technology and assisting other girls who want to leave the company. Apart from being helpful and brave, Jieling is also not a naïve character. Many characters who find themselves in similar roles and circumstances end up being betrayed because they trust the wrong people. In contrast, Jieling is not easily persuaded and she is cautious about trusting strangers.

At last it is important to look at the question of why did the author include this type of character in the story. What function does it serve? Unfortunately, it cannot be said with certainty what McHugh's motifs were for including this type of character. Accordingly, the following are simply some suggestions that might seem plausible. Maybe McHugh wanted to underline the importance of family, values and principles as something to hold onto in a fast-paced society in which an individual is constantly surrounded by numerous stimuli and forced to make many quick decisions. However, McHugh might have also wanted to stress the power of an individual. Jieling manages to stand up to the injustice of the biotechnology company even though her resources were inferior to those of the company. This could be taken as an example of why it is important to educate students in way that would make them more confident to really stand up for their values.

5.2. Baiyue

Baiyue is a shy girl who works together with Jieling at the biotechnology company. In many ways, she represents Jieling's counterpart. Whereas Jieling is confident, impatient and rebellious, Baiyue is a nice and patient girl who wants to do everything right and play after the rules – even though they are unjust. Many other girls at the company have simply accepted their situation by trying to focus on the advantages which the company offers (such as clothes, food, accommodations). Baiyue, however, wants to have her freedom back and she has not lost hope that by regularly saving a little bit of money she will one day be able to buy her freedom and leave the company. Unfortunately, her lack of courage and self-confidence kept her from searching alternative solutions that would help her, but also contradict with the companies' set of rules. However, if Baiyue tries to play after the rules, the company will always find a way to stop people from the leaving the company by simply making adjustments to the rules. Only through Jieling's help, Baiyue manages to overcome her concerns and to gather enough courage to take risks. Even though the two girls are different in many ways, they nonetheless develop a close relationship so that in the end Jieling even calls Baiyue her little sister.

Baiyue's character represents a rather familiar agent which can be also found is a variety of other stories. These characters normally have a good deal of potential, but restrained by their circumstances they cannot live up to their potential. Since these characters are not able to escape their situation on their own they depend on a person who can lead and encourage them. After these characters have found their leader they are always loyal and reliable companions. An easy explanation for the use of this type of character is that the leading and confident character (in this story

Jieling) needs a character whom he or she can lead and help. The same goes vice versa since the unconfident person needs somebody who can give them direction and security. Generally speaking these two characters are a good combination since they often complement each other.

5.3. Mr. Wei Rongyi

This agent represents the conflict between traditional values and the process of modernization. As a patriot and a communist government official, he is suspicious of international companies and wants to cause them harm. He does not even stop at breaking the law in order to damage those companies. In his eyes, he might be thinking that he is doing the right thing. Slowing down the process of modernization would help preserving the old customs and traditions. His strong belief in traditional values is probably the main reason why he is unable to adapt to the change in his country. It is difficult to clearly determine his function in the story. On the one hand, he can be seen as the antagonist of the story, since he represents different values than the protagonist, he tries to manipulate Jieling and even breaks into her room and threatens her. On the other hand, however, he unwillingly helps the two girls with his money and even promised to assist them with their goal to reveal the injustices of the biotechnology company to the public. But he never truly followed up on his promise.

6. Time and Space

The story takes place in modern China a few decades into the future where cellphones can be produced in a few minutes on a shabby market and electric ray cells are used to produce electricity. While living in Shenzhen, Jieling does not only experience all these innovations, but also the consequences of the big epidemy that killed one third of China's population. In the first couple of months after moving to Shenzhen, Jieling often finds herself on the plague trash market where many things of the deceased are being sold. The market evokes the image of a loud, dirty, and unorganized space.

Her circumstances change tremendously after she gets a job at a biotechnology company. From that moment on, she does not have to stay in shabby motels or on the dirty market anymore. Now she can stay in the company's compounds. A stark contrast is illustrated since the company's compounds appear clean, modern and bright. This is not the only contrast McHugh used in her story. Differences between the city and the countryside are also mentioned several times. These contrasts maybe try to increase awareness of the fact that the gap between rich and poor is constantly growing and will still be an issue in the future.

This paragraph illustrates once more why the story appears familiar. Apart from its familiar characters, McHugh used a number of other elements which let to this impression. For example, companies that already exist today such as Walmart and the biotechnology company New Life are mentioned. Other remarks are made concerning the New York Times, Communism and terrorism. It seems as if McHugh tried to underline the importance and power of the media and the newspapers. This becomes evident since the characters rather believe that their situation could be improved by the public influence of the media than by the government. Consequently, McHugh might want to encourage people who find themselves in unjust situations to seek out the media in order to raise public awareness for these injustices.

Considering the aspects above, it can be concluded that McHugh used a familiar setting and time frame. In combination with the familiarity of certain characters McHugh maybe tried to make it easier for the reader to relate to the characters and their problems. Problems which we might also face at some point in the future.

7. Voice

The events and characters of this short story are revealed to reader by Jieling's subjective perspective. Some elements are mentioned more often than others. All this depends on Jieling's attitude towards them. For instance, terror attacks and a war between China and Turkmenistan are mentioned, but Jieling does not pay much attention to these events. Therefore, the reader does not receive any further information about these happenings. Another element that occurs several times in the story are the reference to the Communist Party and Mao. However, it appears that Jieling does not have much respect for the government, politics or communist traditions. She rather trusts the western media such as the New York Times newspaper. In her opinion, the media is the only institution who has enough power to reveal the injustices of international companies. With this McHugh could maybe try to show the importance of free media which is not restricted or influenced by the government.

Another aspect of the story influenced by the voice is its pace. Especially in the beginning of the story, Jieling finds herself in a hurry and without patience. She needs a new phone, but she is already frustrated when she has to wait just a few minutes and looking for a job she does not have time for the recruiter to call her back within the next few hours. These examples show a problem which future generations might face. McHugh might have included this raise awareness of this issue. Since young kids who play games on their phones or tablets grow up with instant gratification these kids are not used to waiting and therefore often become extremely impatient.

Another aspect mentioned is Jieling's attitude towards people from the countryside. Many things from the countryside appear to her as not cool or not up-to-date which is why she prefers living in the city. This was maybe included that there will probably always be some preconceptions or prejudices about other regions and people.

Lastly it will be touched upon the function of the epidemic. This might also serve as a warning since an epidemic could always be an enormous problem for humanity. But the epidemic does not appear to be McHugh's main focus. It is interesting, however, that Jieling shows empathy for Mr Rongyi who had lost his daughter in the epidemic. Jieling can relate to his pain because she had lost her father. This example could be generalized because if something bad happens to another person like an illness or a natural disaster, other people often show empathy. Especially, when something similar had happened to them, their friends or their families.

8. Final thoughts

McHugh's interactive writing style manages to capture the reader and to influence him to use his own imagination. She also creates an easy to follow narrative with some unexpected twist and turns. The characters appear familiar even though only parts of their identity are revealed.

Not only the characters and the story line leave room for discussion, but also the content of the story. Many unanswered questions arise after reading the story. Will the biotechnology company face legal consequences or will the government simply stand by? Already today, the power of global corporations is a problem. There are companies who have the resources to buy entire countries and therefore many governments are either influenced by these companies or they cannot go up against them. As mentioned in the story, Jieling seems to have more hope that the media would be able to do something against the unjust treatment of the company than the government. However, it has to be guaranteed that the media is truly reliable, neutral and honest. Unfortunately, this is not always the case because there are various newspapers who are influenced by the government or other political or personal interests.

Another aspect mentioned in the story which is relevant today is the question about the cost of progress and modernization. In the story, the biotechnology company has to break the law in order to keep up with its competition. There is also the growing gap between rural and urban areas along with the differences between modern values and old traditions.

All these aspects considered, "Special Economics" is definitely a notable example of a contemporary short story and definitely worth reading and discussing.

YOUR KNOWLEDGE HAS VALUE

- We will publish your bachelor's and master's thesis, essays and papers

- Your own eBook and book - sold worldwide in all relevant shops

- Earn money with each sale

Upload your text at www.GRIN.com
and publish for free